REAL ESTATE EXAMPREP

OHIO

Dearborn™
Real Estate Education

While a great deal of care has been taken to provide accurate and current information, the ideas, suggestions, general principles, and conclusions presented in this text are subject to local, state and federal laws and regulations, court cases, and any revisions of same. The reader is urged to consult legal counsel regarding any points of law. This publication should not be used as a substitute for competent legal advice.

Publisher: Evan Butterfield
Senior Development Editor: Kristen Short
Senior Managing Editor: Ronald J. Liszkowski
Art Manager: Lucy Jenkins
Cover Design: Gail Chandler

Exam Prep Series Content Consultant: Marie Spodek, DREI

Copyright 2001 by Dearborn Financial Publishing, Inc.®

Published by Dearborn Real Estate Education®
a division of Dearborn Financial Publishing, Inc.®
155 North Wacker Drive
Chicago, IL 60606-1719
http://www.dearbornRE.com

All rights reserved. The text of this publication, or any part thereof, may not be reproduced in any manner whatsoever without written permission from the publisher.

Printed in the United States of America.

01 02 03 10 9 8 7 6 5 4 3 2 1

Introduction

Welcome to *Ohio Exam Prep*! When you bought this book, you showed that you are serious about passing the exam and getting your real estate license. This is *NOT* an easy test. For people whose test-taking skills are weak, or who haven't adequately prepared, the exam can be a nightmare. For those who have taken the time and effort to study and review, however, the exam can be a much more positive experience.

It's pretty obvious, though, that if you practice and review key material, your test score will improve. This book is your key to exam success.

The process is simple: Just work your way through the practice questions, taking your time and answering each one carefully. Then check your answers by studying the Answer Key, where you'll find both the correct answer to each question as well as an explanation of *why* that answer is correct. It might be a good idea to review your classroom materials and textbook before you start.

Remember: These 200 questions reflect as closely as possible the topic coverage of the state-specific portion of your exam only! For the balance of the test, you'll need to use a "national" exam prep book. And remember, too, that it takes study and hard work on your part to pass the licensing exam: no single study aid will do the trick alone.

Experts who are familiar with the Ohio licensing examination, as well as real estate law and practice, prepared this book. You've taken the first step toward your success as a real estate professional: Good Luck!

Dearborn Real Estate Education

1. A condominium unit is considered to be

   A. personal property.
   B. real property.
   C. commercial property.
   D. common property.

2. The common areas and facilities of a condominium property are owned by the unit owners as

   A. joint tenancy.
   B. tenancy by the entirety.
   C. tenancy in common.
   D. severalty.

3. A condominium unit owners' association is governed by

   A. declarations.
   B. charter.
   C. certificate.
   D. bylaws.

4. How many hours of continuing education must a licensed appraiser complete annually?

   A. 8
   B. 14
   C. 20
   D. 26

5. How many business days does the state have to file a written report once a complaint against a licensed appraiser is filed with the Division of Real Estate?

   A. 30
   B. 60
   C. 90
   D. 120

6. How long must an appraiser retain an appraisal report?

   A. One year
   B. Two years
   C. Three years
   D. Five years

7. Which of the following must hold a current Ohio real estate broker's license?

   A. Administrative assistant
   B. Title insurance agent
   C. Mortgage broker
   D. Property manager

8. In Ohio, the amount of a broker's commission is negotiable in

   A. every case.
   B. commercial transactions only.
   C. residential transactions only.
   D. interstate transactions only.

9. All salespersons and brokers in Ohio must disclose whom they represent to avoid an unintended or undisclosed

   A. fiduciary relationship.
   B. primary agency relationship.
   C. dual agency relationship.
   D. independent contract relationship.

10. Under Ohio law, the process that requires a licensee to provide a full disclosure of all monies in a real estate transaction is called a(n)

    A. disclosure.
    B. accounting.
    C. agency.
    D. brokerage.

11. When a consumer makes a complaint against a licensee, the three-year statute of limitations for the commission and superintendent to commence an investigation begins at the time the complaint is

    A. filed with the DRE.
    B. adjudicated in court.
    C. certified by the superintendent.
    D. occurred or arose.

12. The Ohio Real Estate Commission consists of how many members?

    A. Three
    B. Five
    C. Seven
    D. Nine

13. The Division of Real Estate, which regulates brokers and licensees, is under the supervision of the

    A. director of real estate.
    B. director of state affairs.
    C. director of public utilities.
    D. director of commerce.

14. An application for an Ohio broker's license must be accompanied by how many resident freeholders' references?

    A. Two
    B. Three
    C. Four
    D. Five

15. To sit for the broker's license examination, the applicant must have completed how many real estate transactions?

    A. 10
    B. 15
    C. 20
    D. 25

16. What is the minimum score required to pass the Ohio real estate broker's examination?

    A. 60 percent
    B. 65 percent
    C. 70 percent
    D. 75 percent

17. How many times can an applicant retake the broker's examination in a one-year period?

    A. Three
    B. Five
    C. Seven
    D. An unlimited number of times

18. What amount of the application fee for the salesperson's examination is credited to the real estate education and research fund?

    A. $2.00
    B. $3.00
    C. $4.00
    D. $5.00

19. Ohio law limits the amount of claims filed with the real estate recovery fund against any one salesperson or broker to

    A. $20,000.
    B. $40,000.
    C. $50,000.
    D. $100,000.

20. Real estate licensees must submit proof of having satisfactorily completed 30 classroom hours of approved continuing real estate education every

    A. two years.
    B. three years.
    C. four years.
    D. five years.

21. "Agency" and "agency relationship" are defined by the ORC as the relationship between a licensee and the

    A. superintendent.
    B. general public.
    C. escrow agency.
    D. person whom the licensee represents in a real estate transaction.

22. An "in-company transaction" is defined as a real estate transaction in which the

    A. seller and purchaser are both licensees.
    B. purchaser uses the same escrow agent as the brokerage.
    C. seller uses the same escrow agent as the brokerage.
    D. seller and purchaser are both represented by the same brokerage.

23. Manufactured houses, also known as mobile homes, are considered what type of property in Ohio?

    A. Real
    B. Personal
    C. Residential
    D. Commercial

24. What type of license is required to sell mobile homes in Ohio?

    A. Salesperson's
    B. Broker's
    C. Limited salesperson's
    D. None

25. Ohio courts consider an oral listing agreement to be

    A. binding.
    B. nonbinding.
    C. illegal.
    D. void.

26. Which of the following must be included in a written agency agreement in Ohio?

    A. Broker license number
    B. An expiration date
    C. Escrow instructions
    D. Earnest money disclosure

27. Spousal dower rights in Ohio create an estate for life in real estate in the amount of

    A. 25 percent.
    B. 33 percent.
    C. 40 percent.
    D. 50 percent.

28. Ohio law recognizes which of the following real property rights based upon marriage?

    A. Community property
    B. Curtesy
    C. Dower
    D. Joint tenancy

29. What is the statute of limitations to file an action to recover the title to or possession of real property in Ohio?

    A. 6 years
    B. 10 years
    C. 14 years
    D. 21 years

30. In a real property foreclosure, the debtor may redeem the foreclosed property at any time prior to the

    A. judicial confirmation.
    B. sheriff's sale.
    C. newspaper notice.
    D. foreclosure notice.

31. In the event the foreclosure sale results in more money than is necessary to satisfy the writ of execution and all related expenses, who is entitled to the surplus?

    A. Creditor
    B. Debtor
    C. Sheriff
    D. Court

32. If a licensed real estate broker pays a commission or referral fee to another licensed real estate broker in another state, Ohio law considers this action

    A. legal.
    B. illegal.
    C. void.
    D. criminal.

33. Which of the following is an example of foreign real estate as defined by the Ohio Revised Code?

    A. Real property located in another county in Ohio different from where the licensee practices
    B. Real property in Ohio separated by a national scenic river
    C. Federal land located in Ohio
    D. An option to purchase land anywhere outside of Ohio

34. What is the maximum amount of time a licensee has to return a referral fee when assisting prospective tenants but failing to find rental housing per the client's specifications?

    A. 30 days
    B. 60 days
    C. 90 days
    D. 120 days

35. What is the term of office for members of the Ohio Real Estate Commission?

    A. Two years
    B. Three years
    C. Five years
    D. Seven years

36. What is the maximum number of commission members that can be affiliated with any one political party?

    A. Two
    B. Three
    C. Four
    D. Five

37. What is the minimum number of years of real estate broker experience that four of the five members of the Ohio Real Estate Commission must possess prior to appointment?

    A. Three
    B. Five
    C. Seven
    D. Ten

38. Which of the following is a statutory power and duty of the Ohio Real Estate Commission?

    A. Approving federal civil rights legislation
    B. Passing state statutes relating to real estate practice
    C. Setting standards for appraisers
    D. Adopting Canons of Ethics for the real estate industry

39. What is the proper order of official activities after a written complaint has been filed against a licensed broker or salesperson?

    A. Informal meeting, investigation of complaint, formal hearing, review by commission
    B. Investigation of complaint, formal hearing, informal meeting, review by commission
    C. Review by commission, investigation of complaint, informal meeting, formal hearing
    D. Investigation of complaint, informal meeting, formal hearing, review by commission

40. Which of the following can the Ohio Real Estate Commission impose against a licensed broker or salesperson as a disciplinary sanction?

    A. Restitution
    B. Probation
    C. Reprimand
    D. Parole

41. What is the current application fee for a real estate broker's license?

    A. $39.00
    B. $50.00
    C. $69.00
    D. $75.00

42. What amount of the real estate broker's license is credited to the real estate education and research fund?

    A. $2.00
    B. $4.00
    C. $5.00
    D. $10.00

43. What is the minimum age required to take the Ohio real estate broker's examination?

    A. 16
    B. 18
    C. 20
    D. 21

44. Under what act will reasonable accommodations be made for taking the real estate broker's examination?

    A. Ohio Fair Housing Law
    B. RESPA
    C. Americans with Disabilities Act of 1990
    D. Civil Rights Act of 1964

45. Under which of the following circumstances can the superintendent waive the real estate broker's examination requirement?

    A. If the applicant has held a salesperson's license for at least 30 years
    B. If the applicant is licensed as an attorney in Ohio
    C. If the applicant had a broker's license within two years of the application
    D. If the applicant is at least 70 years old with ten years of experience as a licensed real estate salesperson

46. How many hours of classroom instruction in real estate brokerage must each real estate broker licensee complete?

    A. 10
    B. 15
    C. 20
    D. 30

47. If a broker licensee fails to complete the real estate brokerage educational requirement within the prescribed time period, what disciplinary sanction is imposed by law?

    A. Automatic license revocation
    B. Automatic license suspension
    C. Automatic fine
    D. Automatic probation

48. The application fee for a salesperson's license is

    A. $29.00.
    B. $39.00.
    C. $49.00.
    D. $59.00.

49. What is the maximum number of times an applicant can retake the examination for a real estate salesperson's license?

    A. There is no limit.
    B. Three
    C. Five
    D. Ten

50. How many prelicensure classroom hours of real estate education must an applicant complete prior to taking the Ohio real estate salesperson's examination?

    A. 60
    B. 90
    C. 120
    D. 150

51. How many classroom hours must the salesperson complete within one year of licensure?

    A. 3
    B. 10
    C. 18
    D. 30

52. By what period of time must an applicant for the Ohio salesperson's license complete all educational requirements?

    A. Three years
    B. Five years
    C. Seven years
    D. Ten years

53. What is the maximum amount that a claimant may receive from the real estate recovery fund per licensee?

    A. $25,000.00
    B. $40,000.00
    C. $50,000.00
    D. $60,000.00

54. When a payment from the real estate recovery fund is made to a claimant, the license of a broker or salesperson is automatically

    A. revoked.
    B. suspended.
    C. rejected.
    D. escrowed.

55. A claim filed with the real estate recovery fund may seek what type of damages?

    A. Actual and direct losses
    B. Punitive damages
    C. Judgment interest
    D. Fines

56. An Ohio real estate broker's license must be

    A. carried with the broker when showing property.
    B. prominently displayed in the office or place of business.
    C. placed in a secure place for safekeeping.
    D. attached to every escrow instruction to receive a commission.

57. How many days does a licensee have to notify the superintendent of a felony conviction or other reportable violation?

    A. 5
    B. 7
    C. 10
    D. 15

58. If a licensee is convicted of a violation of any municipal civil rights law pertaining to housing discrimination, which of the following must the court must notify?

    A. Ohio Fair Housing Commission
    B. Ohio Civil Rights Commission
    C. Ohio Real Estate Commission
    D. Department of Housing and Urban Development (HUD)

59. If a licensee enters the armed forces, what options does the licensee have regarding his or her real estate license?

    A. The license can be placed in escrow indefinitely.
    B. The license can be placed on deposit with the Ohio Real Estate Commission until six months after discharge.
    C. The license can remain active as long as all fees are current.
    D. The license can be held by the broker as long as the licensee is on active duty.

60. If a licensee places his or her license on deposit with the Ohio Real Estate Commission while in the armed forces, by what period of time following discharge must the licensee comply with all continuing education requirements?

    A. 6 months
    B. 12 months
    C. 18 months
    D. 24 months

61. If a real estate broker desires to associate himself with another real estate broker in the capacity of a real estate salesperson, what must he do?

    A. Nothing; the broker's license is valid for this purpose.
    B. Take and pass the real estate salesperson's examination
    C. Apply to the superintendent for dual licensure
    D. Place the broker's license on deposit with the superintendent and request the issuance of a salesperson's license

62. How long are the real estate broker's and salesperson's licenses valid?

    A. One year
    B. Three years
    C. Five years
    D. They are valid until canceled, revoked, suspended, or expired by operation of law.

63. If a real estate license is canceled or revoked, in what activity can the licensee engage?

    A. The licensee can practice real estate until all appeals are exhausted.
    B. The licensee can practice real estate only on current contracts.
    C. The licensee can practice real estate only in association with a broker.
    D. The licensee cannot practice real estate.

64. If a license is canceled for failure to file a certificate of continuation, what period of time does the licensee have to reactivate the license?

    A. 6 months
    B. 12 months
    C. 18 months
    D. 36 months

65. How many hours of continuing education must a licensee complete every three years?

    A. 30
    B. 45
    C. 50
    D. 60

66. What period of time does a licensee have to complete mandatory continuing education requirements?

    A. One year
    B. Two years
    C. Three years
    D. Five years

67. Which of the following is a correct statement regarding continuing education course examinations and attendance?

    A. The licensee must be physically present for at least 75 percent of the course.
    B. The licensee must pass a final examination.
    C. The licensee must attend every clock hour of the course.
    D. The licensee must complete a written component of the course.

68. If a licensee does not complete the 30-hour continuing education course requirements every three years, what disciplinary action will occur?

    A. Automatic revocation
    B. Automatic suspension
    C. Automatic fine
    D. Automatic probation

69. If a real estate broker becomes a member or officer of an organization that is or intends to become a licensed real estate brokerage, what action must the broker take?

    A. Revoke his or her license
    B. File a conflict of interest form
    C. Notify the superintendent
    D. Nothing; Ohio only requires that the license be current.

70. If a real estate broker is an officer of a corporation that is also licensed to sell real estate, in what legal capacity is the broker acting for the corporation when he or she sells property?

    A. Principal
    B. Agent
    C. Legal representative
    D. Escrow officer

71. A licensee who is 70 or older is required to complete how many continuing education hours every three years?

    A. 7
    B. 9
    C. 15
    D. 30

72. Who of the following can request an extension of time from the superintendent to complete continuing education requirements?

    A. Agent licensees
    B. Broker licensees
    C. Physically handicapped licensees
    D. 70-year-old licensees

73. If the license of a real estate broker is suspended for failing to meet the required continuing education requirements, the licensee status of any real estate salesperson employed by the broker within the time allotted

    A. is revoked.
    B. is suspended.
    C. is deactivated.
    D. does not change.

74. What is the fee for a branch office license?

    A. $5.00
    B. $8.00
    C. $15.00
    D. $25.00

75. The fee to transfer the license of a real estate salesperson is

    A. $10.00.
    B. $20.00.
    C. $35.00.
    D. $49.00.

76. The fee for a certificate of continuation as a real estate broker is

    A. $10.00.
    B. $20.00.
    C. $35.00.
    D. $49.00.

77. The fee to transfer a broker's license into or out of a partnership, association, or corporation, or from one partnership, association, or corporation to another partnership, association, or corporation is

   A. $10.00.
   B. $20.00.
   C. $25.00.
   D. $39.00.

78. The fee for a foreign real estate salesperson's license in Ohio and each annual renewal of the license is

   A. $25.00.
   B. $50.00.
   C. $75.00.
   D. $100.00.

79. The ORC requires every licensed real estate broker to maintain a definite place of business with a sign on the premise. The sign must indicate

   A. that the licensee is a broker.
   B. the license number of the broker.
   C. the fictitious name of the firm.
   D. the legal name of the firm.

80. If a licensed real estate broker or salesperson advertises to sell, exchange, or lease personally owned real estate, the licensee must disclose in the advertisement

   A. the street address of the licensee's place of business.
   B. the name of the attorney handling the transaction.
   C. his or her name and the type of real estate license he or she possesses.
   D. the commission fee, including the buyer's responsibility.

81. If a licensed real estate salesperson lists her personal real property for sale with her broker, which of the following must be included in the advertisement?

   A. The name of the licensee's broker and his or her status as a broker
   B. The name of the licensee's broker and the broker's principal place of business
   C. The name and license number of the licensee's broker
   D. The name and fee commission of the licensee's broker

82. A real estate salesperson places an ad to promote the sale of his personal residence and includes in the ad the name of his broker. In what size should his broker's name appear?

   A. Larger than the name of the salesperson
   B. Smaller than the name of the salesperson
   C. Equal to the name of the salesperson
   D. Any size

83. Which of the following is a true statement in regard to a real estate salesperson listing his or her personal real property?

    A. A salesperson who does not list personal real property with his or her broker does not have to include the broker's name in the advertisement.
    B. In all advertisements, a salesperson must state his or her name, his or her broker's name, and the license status of each.
    C. Only a broker's name is required in an advertisement when a salesperson lists personal real property for sale with the broker.
    D. Neither the salesperson's nor the broker's name is required to be in any real estate advertising.

84. When must a licensee provide a copy of a listing or other agreement to the signor of the document?

    A. Within ten days
    B. Within five days
    C. Within three days
    D. Immediately

85. In what area of a broker's office must a nondiscrimination statement be displayed?

    A. Where real estate licenses are displayed
    B. Outside the front entrance
    C. In the main conference room
    D. Inside the broker's office

86. Which agency logo must appear in the nondiscrimination statement of broker offices?

    A. U.S. Department of Housing and Urban Development (HUD)
    B. Ohio Civil Rights Commission
    C. Ohio Real Estate Commission
    D. Ohio Department Of Commerce

87. Nonresidents and foreign corporations may hold an Ohio real estate license if they file which of the following documents with their license application?

    A. Current state real estate license
    B. Commercial liability insurance coverage
    C. An irrevocable consent to Ohio suits and actions
    D. Ohio civil rights acknowledgment

88. Who is primarily responsible for investigating the conduct of any real estate licensee?

    A. Director of Commerce
    B. Superintendent
    C. Director of Public Utilities
    D. Ohio Real Estate Disciplinary Commission

89. What period of time must a licensed broker maintain real estate transaction records?

    A. One year
    B. Two years
    C. Three years
    D. Five years

90. What period of time does an interested party have to request that the Ohio Real Estate Commission reverse, vacate, or modify its own orders?

    A. 5 days
    B. 10 days
    C. 15 days
    D. 20 days

91. If a salesperson receives disciplinary sanctions from the Ohio Real Estate Commission, under what circumstance may the salesperson's broker receive disciplinary action?

    A. If the broker had knowledge of the salesperson's action
    B. If the broker is sued civilly for the salesperson's action
    C. If the broker received a commission
    D. If the broker did not seek legal advice

92. Which of the following examples would be considered an illegal commission?

    A. A commission to a licensed real estate broker for a home listing
    B. A commission to a licensed real estate salesperson for a home sale
    C. A commission to a licensed foreign real estate broker for marketing services
    D. A commission to a mortgage broker for a client referral

93. If a real estate broker or foreign real estate dealer's license is suspended or revoked, what happens to the affiliated salesperson's license?

    A. It is automatically revoked.
    B. It is automatically suspended.
    C. It is automatically transferred to the superintendent.
    D. It is not affected.

94. Commissions for the sale of any cemetery lot are determined by the

    A. board of trustees of the cemetery company or association.
    B. Division of Real Estate.
    C. local board of REALTORS®.
    D. Department of Housing and Urban Development.

95. Any person who wants to sell, lease, or otherwise deal in any foreign real estate in Ohio must

    A. post a bond equal to the value of the foreign real property.
    B. file a detailed application with the superintendent of real estate.
    C. obtain a valid Ohio real estate broker's license.
    D. ensure that all real estate transfers are handled by an Ohio escrow agency.

96. In regulating the sale of foreign real estate in Ohio, the superintendent of real estate may require which of the following?

    A. That all payments for foreign real estate be impounded in an Ohio bank
    B. That foreign real estate deeds be recorded in Ohio
    C. That all foreign real estate purchased by Ohioans be guaranteed a 180-day refund
    D. That maximum commission rates for the sale of foreign real estate be established

97. If an application to qualify foreign real estate is refused by the superintendent, how many days after the order can the applicant file a new application?

    A. Three
    B. Five
    C. Seven
    D. Ten

98. How many times can a foreign real estate dealer license applicant take the Ohio examination before waiting six months to retake the examination?

    A. One
    B. Two
    C. Three
    D. Five

99. The licenses of foreign real estate dealers and salespersons expire every

    A. year.
    B. two years.
    C. three years.
    D. four years.

100. What is the statute of limitations for the Ohio Real Estate Commission or the superintendent to commence an investigation for an alleged violation of the ORC?

     A. One year
     B. Two years
     C. Three years
     D. Five years

101. Which of the following regarding written agency agreements is true?

     A. Only written agency agreements are valid in Ohio.
     B. The written agency agreement must be signed at the closing.
     C. The written agency agreement must have an expiration date.
     D. The written agency agreement must be filed with the Superintendent.

102. A licensed foreign real estate salesperson in Ohio may be employed by which of the following?

     A. A licensed real estate broker in Ohio
     B. A licensed real estate salesperson in Ohio
     C. A licensed foreign real estate broker in Ohio
     D. The superintendent of real estate

103. An "affiliated licensee" is defined as a

     A. real estate broker or salesperson from another state.
     B. client who has a suspended license.
     C. real estate broker or salesperson appointed to represent a decedent's estate.
     D. real estate broker or salesperson who is licensed in Ohio and affiliated with an Ohio brokerage.

104. A "subagency" and "subagency relationship" are defined as a relationship in which a licensee

    A. acts for another licensee in performing duties for the client of that licensee.
    B. works directly with the client.
    C. sells his/her own property without a listing agreement.
    D. places his or her license in escrow with the superintendent.

105. A "client" is defined as any person who

    A. might be interested in real estate.
    B. responds to a real estate advertisement.
    C. has entered into an agency relationship with a licensee.
    D. has requested specific information on a listing.

106. The term "purchaser" is defined to include

    A. an agent of a lessor.
    B. lessees.
    C. sellers.
    D. subagents.

107. "Management level licensee" is defined as a licensee who

    A. helps managers in corporate relocations.
    B. is certified to own a brokerage.
    C. is authorized to represent any affiliated licensee.
    D. has supervisory responsibility over other licensees.

108. The types of agency relationships permitted in a real estate transaction are determined by statute and the duties of a real estate agent are determined by

    A. practice.
    B. industry standard.
    C. common law.
    D. market conditions.

109. An agency agreement must include which of the following?

    A. A statement defining the practice of "blockbusting" and stating that it is illegal
    B. A statement defining the practice of "steering" and stating that it is illegal
    C. A statement defining the practice of "switch and bait" and stating that it is illegal
    D. A statement defining the practice of "fraud" and stating that it is illegal

110. An Ohio real estate brokerage must do which of the following where agency relationships are concerned?

    A. Provide all agents with 15 hours of agency law training
    B. Maintain a written company policy establishing what types of agency relationships are allowed
    C. Establish an agency relationship coordinator in each office
    D. Review all agency agreements once a year for redesign and updating

111. Four types of permissible agency relationships are established under the ORC. Which of the following is a correct agency description?

    A. An agency relationship between the seller and purchaser
    B. An agency relationship between the title officer and licensee
    C. An agency relationship between the licensee and the purchaser
    D. An agency relationship between the seller and mortgage banker

112. Which of the following is an example of a dual agency?

    A. A licensee who represents both the seller and purchaser
    B. A licensee who represents the purchaser only
    C. A licensee who represents the seller only
    D. A licensee who represents the escrow agent and seller

113. Which of the following is an example of subagency?

    A. A licensee who represents the brokerage only
    B. A licensee who represents a "for sale by owner" client
    C. A licensee who represents the licensee only
    D. A licensee who represents the client of another licensee

114. Which of the following real estate transactions requires a written agency disclosure agreement?

    A. The sale of a cemetery lot or cemetery interment right
    B. Rental or lease agreements that can be performed in 18 months or less
    C. The referral of a prospective buyer, tenant, seller, or landlord to another licensee
    D. The representation by licensee of both buyer and purchaser

115. When must a licensee who is acting as a seller's agent provide the seller a written agency disclosure statement?

    A. Prior to marketing or showing the seller's property
    B. At the time an offer is presented to the seller
    C. When the earnest money is accepted by the seller
    D. At the closing

116. If the brokerage is acting as a dual agent, which of the following statements should be included in the agency disclosure statement?

    A. That the brokerage and its agents can represent only one client
    B. That the brokerage might represent the separate interest of the buyer and the seller
    C. That the brokerage can only represent the seller
    D. That the brokerage must act in the best interest of all parties

117. If a licensee is representing a buyer exclusively, when must the licensee disclose the buyer agency relationship?

    A. At the first contact with the seller or the seller's licensee representative
    B. At the time a purchase offer is made
    C. At the time a purchase offer is accepted
    D. At the time of closing and commission payment

118. When does a licensee owe a fiduciary duty to a client?

    A. At the first contact with the client
    B. When an agency or subagency is created
    C. When a purchase offer is signed
    D. When seller and purchaser sign a fiduciary disclosure statement

119. Which of the following is a duty owed by the licensee representing a seller?

    A. Presenting only purchase offers the licensee deems acceptable
    B. Presenting all purchase offers in a timely manner to the client
    C. Seeking additional offers until all contingencies have been removed from a signed purchase agreement
    D. Accepting and signing offers on behalf of the seller

120. Which of the following estates was abolished by statute in Ohio?

    A. Curtesy
    B. Dower
    C. Life estate
    D. Tenancy in common

121. Which of the following is not included in the ORC's definition of real estate?

    A. Leaseholds
    B. Land improvements
    C. Freehold estates
    D. Cemetery interment rights

122. Which of the following statements is true of a real estate broker acting as a seller's agent in Ohio?

    A. The broker is obligated to render faithful service to the seller.
    B. The broker can disclose personal information to a buyer if it increases the likelihood of a sale.
    C. The broker can agree to a change in price without the seller's approval.
    D. The broker can accept a commission from the buyer without the seller's approval.

123. Under Ohio law, the agency disclosure statement must be given to prospective purchasers/tenants no later than

    A. the first time they are shown any properties.
    B. at an open house.
    C. at the closing table.
    D. the time any offers to purchase or lease are prepared or presented.

124. After a hearing, the Ohio Real Estate Commission may suspend or revoke the license of a licensee who

    A. has violated any of the provisions of the Ohio license law.
    B. is not a REALTOR®.
    C. is being sued in court.
    D. practicing real estate in a foreign jurisdiction.

125. In Ohio, members of a real estate brokerage business partnership or an association who perform the functions of a real estate broker must

   A. all be licensed brokers.
   B. all be licensed brokers or licensed salespersons.
   C. all be limited real estate dealers or limited real estate salespersons.
   D. Partners or association members do not have to be licensed as brokers or salespersons.

126. A person in the business of collecting and selling information on apartments available for rent

   A. is exempt from the Ohio real estate license law.
   B. must hold an Ohio securities license.
   C. must hold an Ohio real estate broker's license.
   D. must hold an Ohio vendor's license.

127. Which of the following amounts is deducted from the application and renewal fees for real estate licenses?

   A. $10 to further the cause of education and research of real estate at Ohio institutions of higher education
   B. $4 to further the cause of education and research of real estate at Ohio institutions of higher education
   C. $40 to replenish the real estate recovery special account
   D. $10 to replenish the real estate recovery special account

128. A licensee can have his or her Ohio real estate license revoked for

   A. placing a "for sale" sign on a property without the owner's consent.
   B. advertising in the local newspapers.
   C. belonging to a local trade association.
   D. buying a property he or she has listed after having disclosed to the seller, in writing, that he or she holds an Ohio real estate license.

129. An applicant who fails the Ohio broker's or salesperson's licensing exam

   A. may retake the exam as often as needed, with no time limitation.
   B. may take the exam again only after completing a review course.
   C. must wait one full year before sitting for the exam again.
   D. may retake the exam within six months.

130. A salesperson may have his or her license suspended or revoked for

   A. advertising properties in another county.
   B. using a broker's separate account as a depositary for monies received.
   C. paying a finder's fee to an unlicensed person.
   D. completing 30 hours of continuing education in one year.

131. A broker violates the Ohio Revised Code when he or she

    A. operates in his or her own name alone and at the same time as an active member or officer of a licensed partnership or corporation.
    B. associates with another broker as a salesperson.
    C. violates the Code of Ethics of the National Association of REALTORS®.
    D. deposits his or her license with the Ohio Division of Real Estate.

132. In Ohio, the real estate license of a person who willingly disregards or violates any of the provisions of the Ohio real estate license law

    A. will be suspended or revoked.
    B. may not be reissued for six months.
    C. will be suspended for six months.
    D. may be reinstated upon payment of a fine.

133. All Ohio real estate brokers must

    A. be bonded.
    B. display the licenses of their salespeople.
    C. post the equal housing poster in a prominent place in their office.
    D. be either Realtists or REALTORS®.

134. In Ohio, a real estate broker must

    A. list properties.
    B. include his or her name in advertisements of a client's property.
    C. belong to a local trade association.
    D. hold open houses.

135. A real estate licensee who is not an attorney and engages in any activity that constitutes the practice of law

    A. may charge a fee for preparing deeds.
    B. is in violation of the Ohio real estate license law.
    C. may legally do so only in the area of real estate law.
    D. is not acting illegally.

136. Appointments to the Ohio Real Estate Commission are made by the

    A. director of commerce.
    B. superintendent of real estate.
    C. secretary of state.
    D. governor.

137. The Ohio Real Estate Commission is required by law to do which of the following?

    A. Promulgate a Code of Ethics for the real estate industry
    B. Promulgate Canons of Ethics for the real estate industry
    C. Administer the research rotary fund
    D. Direct the superintendent on content, scheduling, instruction and offerings of real estate appraisal courses

138. The superintendent of real estate is

    A. appointed by the director of commerce.
    B. appointed by the governor.
    C. elected at the general election.
    D. appointed to the position for a five-year term.

139. In Ohio, if a written complaint against a licensee is filed, to whom should the complaint be sent?

    A. The governor
    B. The director of commerce
    C. The superintendent
    D. The Division of Real Estate

140. Survivorship tenancy in Ohio is created only when

    A. a survivorship intent is clearly expressed in the deed.
    B. the parties to the deed are husband and wife.
    C. the parties to the deed are related.
    D. the parties to the deed are named as "joint tenants."

141. Partition in Ohio may be effected

    A. voluntarily.
    B. by a court order.
    C. by eminent domain.
    D. by escheat.

142. Partnership in Ohio may be held in a

    A. fictitious name or a registered name.
    B. unregistered name.
    C. registered trademark.
    D. registered service mark.

143. In the sale of new or converted condominium developments in Ohio, the developer and real estate agent must disclose

    A. the significant terms of any financing offered by or through the developer to the purchaser and a five-year projection of annual expenses for operating and maintaining the common areas.
    B. the significant terms of any financing offered by or through the developer to the purchaser and a two-year projection of annual expenses for operating and maintaining the common areas.
    C. nothing.
    D. only the projection of annual expenses for operating and maintaining the common areas.

144. In Ohio, taxes

    A. are not regulated as to the amount that may be levied against a property owner.
    B. do not exist.
    C. are regulated as to the amount that may be levied against a property owner.
    D. are a percentage of the real estates taxes.

145. In Ohio, a mechanic's lienor must file suit within what time period after the owner of the real estate notifies him or her to commence suit?

    A. 30 days.
    B. 45 days.
    C. 40 days.
    D. 60 days.

146. Once a mechanic's lien is filed as a lien on real estate in Ohio, it may continue as a lien on real estate for

    A. one year renewable.
    B. 60 days nonrenewable.
    C. five years renewable.
    D. six years.

147. In Ohio, the county auditor must reappraise all realty in the state every

    A. four years.
    B. six years.
    C. three years.
    D. ten years.

148. In Ohio, real estate sold for delinquent real estate taxes may

    A. not be redeemed by the former owner.
    B. be redeemed by the former owner by payment in full within 30 days after the sale.
    C. be redeemed by the former owner by payment in full before the confirmation of sale.
    D. be redeemed by the former owner by payment in full within two years after the sale.

149. In Ohio, real estate taxes are usually payable

    A. twice a year.
    B. once a year.
    C. monthly.
    D. biannually.

150. The penalty for failure to pay real estate taxes on the due date in Ohio is

    A. 15 percent of the amount due.
    B. 10 percent of the amount due.
    C. 100 percent of the amount due.
    D. 25 percent of the amount due.

151. Special assessments in Ohio are

    A. collected in the same manner as real estate taxes.
    B. deductible on a federal tax return.
    C. not regulated by any governmental agency.
    D. collected on a quarterly basis.

152. When a certificate of judgment is issued by an Ohio court and filed in an Ohio county, it

    A. immediately becomes a lien on all of the debtor's real estate in that county.
    B. immediately becomes a lien on the debtor's real estate anywhere in Ohio.
    C. cannot attach the debtor's real estate.
    D. will become a lien within ten days after filing.

153. The common level of real estate tax assessment (assessed value) in Ohio is

    A. equal to the appraised value.
    B. 35 percent of the appraised value.
    C. 35 percent of the selling price.
    D. 10 percent of the appraised value.

154. In Ohio, the statutory period for adverse possession is an uninterrupted period of

    A. 30 years.
    B. 7 years.
    C. 3 years.
    D. at least 21 years.

155. Which of the following government entities establishes the Ohio transfer fee rate?

    A. Townships
    B. Villages
    C. Cities
    D. Counties

156. A deed that is signed, witnessed, acknowledged, and certified

   A. passes title.
   B. passes no legal title.
   C. is void.
   D. is illegal.

157. The Ohio transfer fee applies to

   A. gifts between spouses.
   B. the conveyance of real estate.
   C. the conveyance of personal property.
   D. the conveyance of residential property only.

158. To be valid, every will executed in Ohio must be signed by

   A. the testator and witnesses.
   B. a notary public.
   C. the grantor.
   D. the mortgagee.

159. The tax levied based on the purchase price of real property is known as the

   A. county transfer fee.
   B. state conveyance fee.
   C. federal conveyance fee.
   D. state tax.

160. Deeds conveying Ohio real estate require the signature of the

   A. grantor and grantee.
   B. grantor only.
   C. grantee only.
   D. attorney who prepared the deed.

161. Ohio's transfer fee is

   A. $.10 per $100 of total consideration.
   B. $10 per $100 of total consideration.
   C. $.40 per $100 of total consideration.
   D. $1 per $100 of total consideration.

162. A title search in the public records may be conducted by

   A. anyone.
   B. attorneys and abstractors only.
   C. attorneys, abstractors, and real estate licensees only.
   D. anyone who obtains a court order under the Freedom of Information Act.

163. B lives in northern Ohio. Which form of title report is B most likely to use?

   A. Chain of title
   B. Title guaranty
   C. Torrens certificate
   D. Abstract

164. In Ohio the county recorder must determine before recording whether the

   A. permanent parcel number is correct.
   B. signature on the instrument is genuine.
   C. form conforms to Ohio statute.
   D. legal description is correct.

165. To be recognized by third parties in Ohio, a mortgage must be

   A. notarized.
   B. recorded.
   C. witnessed.
   D. registered.

166. It is convenient to record a mortgage on Ohio land

   A. but it is not necessary to create a lien.
   B. so it can be recognized by third parties.
   C. because if it is not recorded, the mortgagor does not have to pay it off.
   D. because if it is not recorded, the mortgagee does not have to pay it off.

167. The recording of a deed in Ohio requires the signatures of the grantor and the

   A. grantee.
   B. notary public who acknowledged the grantor's signature.
   C. attorney who prepared the deed.
   D. witness and notary public who acknowledged the grantor's signature.

168. Under Ohio law, when does a mortgage take effect?

   A. At the same time as in most other states
   B. When delivered to the mortgagee
   C. When delivered to the county recorder
   D. Any time prior to recording

169. Ohio recognizes the right of redemption

   A. for two years after confirmation of the foreclosure sale.
   B. until the foreclosure sale is confirmed after the successful bidding at the sheriff's sale.
   C. for one year after confirmation of the foreclosure sale.
   D. neither before nor after the foreclosure sale.

170. If an Ohio lease is executed properly, the lessee is in possession, and the term is for two years, then the lease

   A. is invalid.
   B. must be recorded.
   C. need not be recorded.
   D. is considered a commercial lease.

171. In Ohio, a landlord may enter leased premises to make repairs if he or she

   A. knocks first to give notice of intent to enter.
   B. gives 24 hours' notice of intent to enter.
   C. gives 48 hours' notice of intent to enter.
   D. enters without knocking.

172. When a residential rental agreement is terminated in Ohio, the landlord must return the tenant's security deposit and provide an itemized list of any deductions for damages

   A. within 30 days after the tenant has vacated the premises; however, the tenant must provide the landlord with an address where the deposit may be mailed.
   B. within 10 days after the tenant has vacated the premises.
   C. even if the landlord does not know where to send the returned deposit.
   D. within 45 days after the tenant has vacated the premises.

173. If, after notice, a landlord fails to remedy a violation of the Ohio Landlord-Tenant Act, the tenant may

   A. refuse to pay further rent.
   B. deposit the withheld rent with the clerk of courts.
   C. deposit the withheld rent in escrow at the bank.
   D. withhold rent until the violation is corrected.

174. In Ohio, a real estate appraiser
    A. must be licensed by the state.
    B. must pass a written examination and be certified.
    C. may or may not be licensed or certified.
    D. may be licensed or certified without taking an examination.

175. A state-licensed residential real estate appraiser may appraise which of the following types of property?
    A. All types of real property located in the state of Ohio
    B. Noncomplex one- to four-unit single-family residential real estate valued at less than $1 million
    C. Complex one- to four-unit single-family residential real estate valued at more than $250,000
    D. Any residential real property located in the county in which the appraiser resides

176. An appraisal is valid
    A. for 60 days.
    B. on the day it is made.
    C. for six months.
    D. for one year.

177. "I hear they're moving in. There goes the neighborhood! Better put your house on the market before values drop!" This is an example of
    A. steering.
    B. blockbusting.
    C. redlining.
    D. testing the market.

178. Which of the following statements is true regarding the Ohio Civil Rights Commission?
    A. It comprises seven members appointed by the governor.
    B. It has no more than four members of the same political party.
    C. It hears complaints filed before it of events that occurred within the 12-month period preceding filing for the complaint.
    D. It attempts to induce noncompliance with the law.

179. Which of the following statements is true of real estate closings in Ohio?
    A. Closings are generally conducted by real estate salespersons.
    B. The buyer usually receives the rents for the day of closing.
    C. The buyer must reimburse the seller for any title evidence provided by the seller.
    D. The seller usually pays the rent expenses through the day of closing.

180. In Ohio, water bills
    A. are not collectible with real estate taxes.
    B. may become a lien on the property and should be collected from the seller.
    C. are "forgiven" when title transfers; this is a gift from the city.
    D. do not have to be paid.

181. Which of the following is prohibited by licensees representing sellers in an agency relationship?

    A. Seeking purchase offers
    B. Presenting any purchase offer
    C. Extending an offer of subagency to other licensees
    D. Negotiating offers in favor of seller

182. A licensee is not liable to any party for false information the licensee's client provided and in turn was passed on to a third party unless the licensee

    A. did not carry professional liability insurance.
    B. was in a dual agency relationship with seller and buyer.
    C. speculated that the information was false.
    D. had actual knowledge that the information was false.

183. Which of the following regarding agency relationships is true?

    A. A licensee may assist a nonclient by providing limited legal advice.
    B. A licensee may assist a nonclient by providing information about lenders, inspectors, and attorneys.
    C. A licensee may assist a nonclient by providing limited, confidential information about a current client.
    D. A licensee cannot help a nonclient in any way.

184. A licensee shall disclose to any purchaser all material facts pertaining to the physical condition of the property when the licensee has what kind of knowledge of these facts?

    A. Incidental knowledge
    B. Speculative knowledge
    C. Actual knowledge
    D. Hearsay knowledge

185. Material facts pertaining to the physical condition of real property may be implied to the licensee if the licensee acts with

    A. reckless disregard for the truth.
    B. knowledge of patent defects.
    C. knowledge of overt defects.
    D. knowledge of obvious defects.

186. If the licensee honestly and fairly discloses material facts pertaining to the condition of the real property to a potential buyer, who may bring a cause of action against the licensee?

    A. The seller
    B. The purchaser
    C. Potential purchasers
    D. No one

187. Regarding disclosure of material physical conditions of real property, the licensee is not required to discover

    A. latent defects.
    B. patent defects.
    C. obvious defects.
    D. outstanding defects.

188. When must the licensee verify the accuracy or completeness of statements made by the seller?

   A. At all times
   B. Only when statements regarding the real property are made
   C. When statements regarding material conditions of the real property are made
   D. No statements must be verified unless the licensee reasonably suspects the accuracy of the statements.

189. Which of the following parties must have full knowledge and consent in writing to dual representation?

   A. The seller
   B. The buyer
   C. Both the seller and buyer
   D. No one; consent can be given verbally

190. When may the seller and buyer revoke their consent in a dual agency relationship?

   A. At any time
   B. At any time prior to signing a purchase agreement
   C. At any time prior to passing title
   D. Only when there is a material change in the information disclosed

191. At what time must the dual agency disclosure statement be signed and dated?

   A. Prior to the signing of purchase offers or leases
   B. After the signing of purchase offers or leases
   C. At the time financing or the down payment is received
   D. At the time title is transferred or the lease is effective

192. Who is responsible for establishing the contents of the dual agency disclosure agreement?

   A. Management-level licensees
   B. Individual brokerage firms
   C. The superintendent of real estate
   D. The Ohio Civil Rights Commission

193. Which of the following must be included in a dual agency disclosure statement?

   A. The material and physical conditions of the real property
   B. The source of compensation to the real estate broker
   C. The financial qualifications of seller and purchaser
   D. The chain of title of the subject property

194. Which of the following post-transaction duties must the licensee provide to a client?

   A. Providing an accounting of all monies relating to the transaction
   B. Providing a limited warranty on certain material conditions
   C. Investigating any complaint against the licenscc's client
   D. Filing tax information relating to the transaction

195. If an applicant is found guilty of knowingly making a false representation for the purpose of qualifying foreign real estate for sale in Ohio, what penalty applies?

   A. Guilty of a misdemeanor and a fine
   B. Guilty of a felony and a fine
   C. Guilty of an infraction but no fine
   D. No criminal sanctions apply.

196. Which of the following is a true statement regarding the licensees duty of confidentiality after the real estate transaction has been completed?

    A. The licensee may discuss any aspect of the deal to anyone.
    B. The licensee may discuss only financial aspects of the deal to anyone.
    C. The licensee may discuss any information the client permits.
    D. The licensee may discuss any information the broker permits.

197. In reference to dual agency disclosure statements, "material relationship" means which of the following?

    A. Any significant condition of the real property
    B. Any marital relationship that may affect dower rights
    C. Any personal, familial, or business relationship between the seller and purchaser
    D. Any personal, familial, or business relationship between a licensee and client that may negatively affect another licensee's client

198. Which of the following is a duty of the brokerage and management-level licensees in a dual agency relationship?

    A. Ensuring that affiliated licensees fulfill their duties/obligations to their clients
    B. Ensuring that affiliated licensees provide equal information to clients and nonclients
    C. Establishing maximum commission rates to protect clients
    D. Providing equal amounts of advertising to be fair to all clients

199. To acknowledge a deed, mortgage, land contract, or lease in Ohio how many people must witness the signing and subscribe their names to the attestation?

    A. One
    B. Two
    C. Three
    D. None--only the transferring parties' signatures are required.

200. Recorded instruments in Ohio must contain

    A. a metes-and-bounds description.
    B. the grantor's and grantee's signatures.
    C. the volume and page reference to the deed.
    D. longitude and latitude.

201. Which of the following best describes the term "root of title"?

    A. The conveyance of ownership in the chain of title providing marketable title
    B. Title to real property that is rooted in a stray deed
    C. Title to real property that has been lost in the chain of title
    D. An improperly recorded title conveying no legal interest

202. What is the effective date of the "root of title"?

    A. The day the grantor signs the deed
    B. The day the grantee signs the deed
    C. The day the grantee receives the signed deed
    D. The day the deed is recorded

203. In Ohio, how many years must an unbroken chain of title of record exist to establish the presumption of marketable record title?

    A. 25
    B. 40
    C. 50
    D. 75

204. Any notice filed in reference to real property must be filed with which of the following agencies?

    A. Division of Real Estate
    B. County auditor
    C. County recorder
    D. County treasurer

205. Which of the following statutory forms of land conveyance in Ohio transfers all real property interests to the remaining holders of title?

    A. General warranty deed
    B. Limited warranty deed
    C. Survivorship tenancy deed
    D. Quitclaim deed

206. Which of the following parties must complete and sign a property disclosure form?

    A. Seller
    B. Buyer
    C. Agent
    D. Broker

207. Which of the following is a true statement regarding a real property disclosure form?

    A. The statement is a warranty of the condition of the real property.
    B. The statement is a substitute for any property inspections.
    C. The statement is a representation of the condition of the property by the agent.
    D. The statement constitutes a statement of the conditions of the property by its sellers.

208. Completion of the real property disclosure form requires that the transferor have

    A. speculative knowledge of the disclosed material condition.
    B. actual knowledge of the disclosed material condition.
    C. extraordinary knowledge of the disclosed material condition.
    D. professional knowledge of the disclosed material condition.

209. After the transferor provides the real property disclosure form to the transferee, what period of time does the transferee have to rescind the property transfer agreement?

    A. Three business days
    B. Five business days
    C. Seven business days
    D. Ten business days

210. Which of the following material matters relating to the physical condition of the property should be included on the real property disclosure form?

    A. Peeling paint on the exterior of the home
    B. Wear and tear on the living room carpet
    C. Leaks in the roof only during very heavy rains
    D. Outdated fixtures in the kitchen

211. Except for statutory liens, when does a lien affect the title to registered land?

    A. When the lien arises
    B. When the lien is noted upon the certificate of title
    C. When the lien is certified by a competent court
    D. When the lien is collected by the claimant

212. Which of the following has the highest priority of claims on registered certificates of title in Ohio?

    A. A private transfer between grantor and grantee
    B. An unrecorded contract for deed sale
    C. Any lien or memorial already recorded against the title
    D. Any lien or memorial agreed to but not recorded against the title

213. What is the primary purpose of the assurance fund in Ohio?

    A. To assure equity ownership by registration of title
    B. To provide right of action for title loss or damage based on fraud or mistake
    C. To pay title insurance to customers of bankrupt title insurance companies
    D. To pay for unsatisfied personal property judgments

214. What is the maximum amount of damages the assurance fund is liable for after a fiscal judgment is entered?

    A. The contract value of the real estate at the time of loss
    B. The listing value of the real estate at the time of loss
    C. The appraised value of the real estate at the time of loss
    D. The fair market value of the real estate at the time of loss

215. Which of the following determines whether land registration (sometimes called Torrens land) will be maintained?

    A. Division of Real Estate
    B. Board of county commissioners
    C. County recorder
    D. Clerk of courts

216. What is the status of registered land after abolition of land registration by the board of county commissioners?

    A. Registered land remains through a grandfather clause.
    B. Registered land remains but has two separate deeds.
    C. Registered land remains although not transferable.
    D. Registered land is re-recorded in the traditional recordation system.

217. Within what period of time must the vendor file a signed land installment contract with both the county recorder and the county auditor?

    A. Within 30 days after both parties have signed the land contract
    B. Within 5 days after both parties have signed the land contract
    C. Within 10 days after both parties have signed the land contract
    D. Within 20 days after both parties have signed the land contract

218. If the landlord fails to fulfill any obligation imposed by Ohio law, which of the following remedies are available to the tenant?

    A. The tenant may stop paying rent until the condition is satisfied.
    B. The tenant may deposit all subsequent rent that is due with the court.
    C. The tenant may file a certificate on noncompliance with the DRE.
    D. The tenant may file a quiet title action against the landlord.

219. If the landlord fails to fulfill any obligation imposed by Ohio law, the tenant may

    A. lock the landlord out of the rental property.
    B. repair the premises and bill the landlord.
    C. terminate the rental agreement.
    D. refuse to pay rent until the habitable conditions are fixed.

220. How many units must a landlord have under rental agreement before a tenant can elect to withhold rent?

    A. One unit
    B. Two units
    C. Three units
    D. Four units

221. A clause in a residential rental agreement providing to pay attorney's fees of either the landlord or tenant are

    A. enforceable.
    B. enforceable, if consideration passes.
    C. unenforceable.
    D. unenforceable, unless attorney's fees exceed $1,000.00.

222. Which of the following is a statutory obligation of a landlord who is a party to a rental agreement?

    A. Providing telephone service
    B. Providing hot and cold water
    C. Providing a garage or other storage areas
    D. Providing cable or satellite service

223. According to the ORC, a permanently sited manufactured home can be built only in

    A. a commercially zoned district.
    B. an industrially zoned district.
    C. an agriculturally zoned district.
    D. any zoned area where single-family homes are permitted.

224. Which of the following agencies is required to maintain a record of plats?

    A. County auditor
    B. County treasurer
    C. County recorder
    D. County commissioners

225. Which of the following agencies is responsible for sending tax statements to all owners of record of real property within the county?

    A. County auditor
    B. County treasurer
    C. County recorder
    D. County commissioners

226. Which of the following agencies may levy a real property transfer tax?

    A. County auditor
    B. County recorder
    C. County treasurer
    D. County commissioners

227. A township board of zoning appeals is permitted to do which of the following?

    A. Issue building permits
    B. Issue eminent domain orders
    C. Issue variances
    D. Issue zoning amendments

228. The process by which a municipal corporation may expand its territory is called

    A. annexation.
    B. compilation.
    C. expansion.
    D. inversion.

229. The ORC defines a plat as

    A. the division of any parcel of land.
    B. a map of a tract or parcel of land.
    C. the valuation and taxation of a parcel of land.
    D. the planning of improvements on a parcel of land.

230. The municipal corporation or neighboring property owners may sue a property owner for zoning violation seeking a(n)

    A. injunction.
    B. criminal prosecution.
    C. property forfeiture action.
    D. deed revocation action.

231. If a subcontractor, laborer, or materialman performs labor or furnishes material and no payment is received, he or she can file a

    A. mortgage lien.
    B. contractor's lien.
    C. mechanic's lien.
    D. facilities lien.

232. A mechanics lien on a single family residence must be filed within 60 days from the

    A. start of the improvement.
    B. midpoint of the improvement.
    C. completion of the improvement.
    D. date the last labor or material was furnished.

233. A mortgage broker is a licensed activity requiring a

    A. real estate salesperson's license.
    B. real estate broker's license.
    C. certificate of registration.
    D. foreign real estate broker's license.

234. When is the mortgage broker entitled to a fee?

    A. At the time of mortgage application
    B. At the time of a listing agreement
    C. At the time of a purchase agreement
    D. At the time the mortgage loan proceeds are disbursed

235. What must a mortgage broker include in advertisements?

    A. Certificate of registration number
    B. HUD disclosure form
    C. Nondiscrimination statement
    D. Specific for disclosure

236. Disciplinary action against a mortgage broker will be filed by the

    A. director of commerce.
    B. superintendent of financial institutions.
    C. superintendent of real estate.
    D. Ohio Real Estate Commission.

237. A power of attorney for the conveyance of real property in Ohio must

    A. be oral.
    B. be coupled with consideration.
    C. acknowledged.
    D. provide a damages clause.

238. A real estate investment trust, before transacting business in Ohio, must file a report with the

    A. Ohio Civil Rights Commission.
    B. Ohio Real Estate Commission.
    C. Ohio Secretary of State.
    D. Ohio Auditor's Office.

239. An owner's/landlord's forcible entry and detainer action must be brought within

    A. one year after the cause of action accrues.
    B. two years after the cause of action accrues.
    C. three years after the cause of action accrues.
    D. five years after the cause of action accrues.

240. An applicant for a residential real estate appraiser certificate or residential real estate appraiser license must have how many years of appraisal experience?

    A. 6 months
    B. 12 months
    C. 18 months
    D. 24 months

241. The real estate appraisal board consists of how many members?

    A. Three
    B. Five
    C. Six
    D. Seven

242. How many hours of continuing education must a real estate appraisal certificate holder and licensee complete within one year immediately following issuance of certificate/license?

    A. 10 hours
    B. 14 hours
    C. 20 hours
    D. 30 hours

243. Who is responsible for assessing real property for taxation purposes?

    A. County auditor
    B. County treasurer
    C. County recorder
    D. County commissioners

244. Who of the following must sign a residential property disclosure form?

    A. Real estate salesperson
    B. Real estate broker
    C. Seller
    D. Appraiser

245. Who of the following must approve the use of brokerage business names?

    A. Superintendent of real estate
    B. Director of commerce
    C. Secretary of state
    D. Ohio Real Estate Commissioner

246. With regard to continuing education requirements, the classroom clock hour consists of at least

    A. 30 minutes.
    B. 45 minutes.
    C. 60 minutes.
    D. 70 minutes.

247. Who of the following may establish regulations regarding planned-unit developments?

    A. The director of commerce
    B. The superintendent of real estate
    C. The Ohio Real Estate Commission
    D. The county board of commissioners

248. Which of the following is an obligation of the tenant in a rental agreement?

    A. Paying all personal consumer credit on time
    B. Keeping the occupied premises safe and sanitary
    C. Maintaining hobbies outside of the rental dwelling
    D. Not declaring bankruptcy during the tenancy

249. If the landlord and the tenant enter into a month-to-month periodic tenancy, how much notice is required to terminate the tenancy under Ohio law?

    A. At least 10 days
    B. At least 20 days
    C. At least 30 days
    D. At least 60 days

250. In the event the tenant commits a prohibited act under the ORC, what period of time must the landlord give the tenant to terminate the rental agreement and vacate the premises?

    A. 3 days
    B. 5 days
    C. 10 days
    D. 30 days

ANSWER KEY

1. B is the correct answer. ORC 5311.03 deems condominium units to be real property.

2. C is the correct answer. ORC 5311.04 states that ownership of common areas and facilities is tenancy in common.

3. D is the correct answer. ORC 5311.08 provides that a unit owners' association is governed by the bylaws.

4. B is the correct answer. ORC 4763.07 requires appraisal licensees and certificate holders to satisfy 14 hours of continuing education every year.

5. B is the correct answer. ORC 4763.11 requires an investigator to file a written report of the results of the investigation with the superintendent within 60 business days.

6. D is the correct answer. The ORC requires appraisers to retain the original appraisal report or a true copy for a period of five years.

7. D is the correct answer. According to ORC 4735.01(A)(5), the functions of a property manager (for example, negotiating leases) are real estate activities that require a broker's license.

8. A is the correct answer. In Ohio, all commissions for real-estate related transactions are negotiable.

9. C is the correct answer. ORC 4735.56 requires upfront disclosures to clients to avoid any misunderstandings about agency relationships.

10. B is the correct answer. ORC 4735.62(H) requires that a licensee must account in a timely manner for all monies and property received in which the client has or may have an interest.

11. A is the correct answer. ORC 4735.32 states that an investigation is considered to be commenced as of the date on which a person files a complaint with the Division of Real Estate.

12. B is the correct answer. ORC 4735.03 provides for five members on the Ohio Real Estate Commission, appointed by the governor.

13. D is the correct answer. ORC 4735.05(A) states that the Ohio Real Estate Commission is a part of the Department of Commerce for administrative purposes. The DRE is under the commission.

14. B is the correct answer. ORC 4735.06(A) requires an application for broker's license to include the names of three resident freeholders of the county in which the applicant resides or has a place of business.

15. C is the correct answer. ORC 4735.07(B)(5)(a) requires applicants to have completed at least 20 real estate transactions before applying for a real estate broker's license.

16. D is the correct answer. ORC 4735.08(A)(1) states that a broker must receive a grade of 75% or better to pass the real estate broker's examination.

17. D is the correct answer. According to ORC 4735.07(F), no limit shall be placed on the number of times an applicant may retake the real estate broker's examination.

18. C is the correct answer. ORC 4735.09(B) states that $4.00 of each application fee shall be credited to the real estate education and research fund.

19. B is the correct answer. ORC 4735.12(D) states that the liability of the fund shall not exceed $40,000 for any one licensee.

20. B is the correct answer. ORC 4735.141(A) requires real estate licensees to satisfactorily complete 30 hours of approved real estate continuing education every three years. The 30 hours of education must be completed on or before the licensee's birthday occurring three years after the licensee's date of initial licensure, and on or before the licensee's birthday every three years thereafter.

21. D is the correct answer. According to ORC 4735.51(A), the terms "agency" and "agency relationship" refer to a relationship in which a licensee represents another person in a real estate transaction.

22. D is the correct answer. ORC 4735.51(I) defines an "in-company transaction" as a real estate transaction in which both the purchaser and seller are represented by the same brokerage.

23. B is the correct answer. Unless permanently sited, Ohio case law characterizes mobile homes as personal property; therefore, no deed is issued to establish ownership.

24. D is the correct answer. Ohio case law has established mobile homes as personal property; therefore, no real estate license is required to sell them.

25. A is the correct answer. Ohio case law establishes that oral listing agreements that do not violate the statute of frauds are enforceable.

26. B is the correct answer. According to ORC 4735.55, a written agency agreement must contain an expiration date in addition to a statement of fair housing laws, the definition of blockbusting, and a copy of the HUD logo.

27. B is the correct answer. ORC 2103.02 provides that a spouse is entitled to one-third of the real property of which the spouse was seized as an estate of inheritance at any time during the marriage.

28. C is the correct answer. ORC 2103.02 establishes dower rights in real property resulting from the marital estate.

29. D is the correct answer. ORC 2305.04 states that an action to recover the title to or possession of real property shall be brought within 21 years after the cause of action has accrued.

30. A is the correct answer. ORC 2329.33 allows the debtor to redeem foreclosed real property any time before judicial confirmation of the sale.

31. B is the correct answer. ORC 2329.44 provides that the clerk of court shall return any remaining balance to the judgment debtor.

32. A is the correct answer. ORC 1301:5-5-06 allows commissions and referral fees to be paid to out of state licensed real estate brokers.

33. D is the correct answer. ORC 4735.01(E) defines foreign real estate as property not situated in Ohio and any interest in real estate not situated in Ohio.

34. B is the correct answer. ORC 4735.021 requires the licensee to return fees to clients no sooner than 30 days but no later than 60 days.

35. C is the correct answer. ORC 4735.03 states that commission members are appointed by the governor with consent of the senate for a term of five years, commencing on July 1.

36. B is the correct answer. According to ORC 4735.03, no more than three of the commission's five members may be members of any one political party.

37. D is the correct answer. ORC 4735.03 requires that four of the commission's five members have at least ten years of real estate broker experience prior to appointment.

38. D is the correct answer. ORC 4735.03 establishes seven responsibilities for the commission, the first of which is adopting Canons of Ethics for the real estate industry.

39. A is the correct answer. According to ORC 47.35051, the DRE must follow the official process when a complaint is filed: informal meeting, investigation of complaint, formal hearing, review by commission.

40. C is the correct answer. ORC 4735.051(H)(4) provides the commission with five disciplinary sanctions: revocation, suspension, fine, reprimand, and additional education.

41. C is the correct answer. According to ORC 4735.06(B), the application fee for a real estate broker's license is $69.00.

42. B is the correct answer. ORC 4735.06(C) provides that $4.00 of each fee for a real estate broker's license shall be credited to the real estate education and research fund. The fund is used by the commission to (1) encourage education and research in real estate and (2) make loans of no more than $500 to real estate salesperson applicants.

43. B is the correct answer. ORC 4735.07(B)(4) requires all applicants for the real estate brokers exam to be at least 18 years of age.

44. C is the correct answer. ORC 4735.07(D) requires that all examinations be in writing although reasonable accommodations under the Americans with Disabilities Act of 1990 shall be provided.

45. C is the correct answer. As provided in ORC 4735.07(G), the superintendent may waive the examination requirement if the applicant was a licensed broker at some time during the two-year period immediately preceding the date of the current application.

46. A is the correct answer. ORC 4735.07(H)(1) requires each real estate broker licensee to complete ten hours of instruction in real estate brokerage within 12 months of obtaining a broker's license. The real estate brokerage course must cover current issues in managing a real estate company or office.

47. B is the correct answer. According to ORC 4735.09(H)(1)(6), if a broker licensee fails to complete the ten hours of brokerage instruction within 12 months of receiving his or her license, the broker's license will be automatically suspended.

48. C is the correct answer. ORC 4735.09(B) requires that a fee of $49.00 accompany the application; the fee shall include the license if it is issued.

49. A is the correct answer. As outlined in ORC 4735.09(C), no limit shall be placed on the number of times an applicant may retake the examination for a real estate salesperson's license.

50. C is the correct answer. ORC 4735.09(6)(a) requires salesperson applicants to complete 120 hours of classroom instruction equally divided between real estate practice, finance, appraisal, and law.

51. B is the correct answer. ORC 4735.09(G) requires salesperson licensees to complete ten hours of classroom instruction in real estate courses that cover current issues regarding consumers, real estate practice, ethics, and real estate law within one year of licensure.

52. D is the correct answer. ORC 4735.09(F)(6)(b) requires that all classroom instruction be successfully completed within a ten-year period immediately preceding the person's current application for the salesperson's examination.

53. B is the correct answer. ORC 4735.12(D) provides that the liability of the fund shall not exceed $40,000.00 per licensee.

54. B is the correct answer. ORC 4735.12(E) provides that upon payment from the fund, licensure is automatically suspended.

55. A is the correct answer. ORC 4735.12(B)(1)8(2) provides that the fund will pay only the portion of the judgment that remains unpaid and that represents the actual and direct loss sustained by the claimant.

56. B is the correct answer. ORC 4735.13(A) requires the license of a real estate broker to be prominently displayed in the broker's office or place of business.

57. D is the correct answer. ORC 4735.13(C) requires licensees to notify all reportable violations to the superintendent within 15 days.

58. B is the correct answer. ORC 4735.12(C) requires the court to notify the Ohio Civil Rights Commission within 15 days of any convictions relating to civil rights housing discrimination.

59. B is the correct answer. ORC 4735.13(G) provides that licensees may place their licenses on deposit with the commission until six months after discharge from the armed services. There is a $7.00 fee for this service.

60. B is the correct answer. ORC 4735.13(G) provides that a licensee who serves in the armed forces with his or her license on deposit with the commission has 12 months to comply with all continuing education requirements.

61. D is the correct answer. ORC 4735.13(E) allows the broker to request from the superintendent that his broker's license be placed on deposit and that a real estate salesperson's license be issued to him. The license deposit fee is $13.00 and the salesperson's license fee is $25.00.

62. D is the correct answer. According to ORC 4735.14, all licenses are valid without further recommendation or examination until canceled, revoked, suspended, or expired by operation of law.

63. D is the correct answer. ORC 4735.14(C) stipulates that no person, partnership, association, corporation, limited liability company or limited partnership shall engage in any act or acts for which a real estate license is required while that entity's license is canceled or revoked.

64. B is the correct answer. ORC 4735.14(C) states that a canceled license may be reactivated within one year of cancellation, provided that the renewal fee plus a penalty fee of 50 percent of the renewal fee is paid to the superintendent.

65. A is the correct answer. ORC 4735.141(A) provides that a licensee must satisfactorily complete 30 classroom hours every three years.

66. C is the correct answer. According to ORC 4735.141, a licensee must complete 30 hours of continuing education within three years of licensure and every three years thereafter, before the licensee's birthday.

67. C is the correct answer. According to ORC 4735.131(A), a continuing education instructor may provide examinations for course evaluation purposes; however, passage is not a continuing education requirement.

68. B is the correct answer. If brokers and salespersons do not complete the 30-hour continuing education course requirements every three years, their real estate licenses will be automatically suspended according to ORC 4735.141(C); no action by the superintendent is required.

69. C is the correct answer. ORC 4735.13(F) requires a broker to notify the superintendent if he or she becomes an officer or member of a partnership, association or corporation that is or intends to become a licensed real estate brokerage.

70. B is the correct answer. According to ORC 4735.13(F), no real estate broker who is a member or officer of a partnership, association, or corporation that is a licensed real estate brokerage shall perform any acts as a real estate broker other than as an agent.

71. B is the correct answer. ORC 4735.14(A) requires licensees 70 or older to complete nine hours of continuing education every three years.

72. C is the correct answer. ORC 4735.14(E) provides that any licensee who is physically handicapped at any time during the last three months of the third year of the licensee's continuing education reporting period may receive an extension of time.

73. B is the correct answer. If the license of a real estate broker is suspended for failing to comply with continuing education requirements, the licenses of any associated salesperson are also suspended per ORC 4735.14(D).

74. B is the correct answer. According to ORC 4735.15(A), the fee for a branch office license is $8.00.

75. B is the correct answer. According to ORC 4735.15(C), the fee to transfer a license by a real estate salesperson is $20.00.

76. D is the correct answer. According to ORC 4735.15, the fee for a certificate of continuation in the business as a real estate broker is $49.00.

77. C is the correct answer. ORC 4735.15 states that the fee to transfer a broker's license into or out of partnership, association, or corporation is $25.00.

78. B is the correct answer. ORC 4735.16(H) provides that the fee for a foreign real estate salesperson's license and each annual renewal of the license is $50.00.

79. A is the correct answer. ORC 4735.16(A) provides that every licensed real estate broker shall have and maintain a definite place of business and shall erect or maintain a sign on the premises plainly stating that the licensee is a real estate broker.

80. C is the correct answer. ORC 4735.16 provides that any licensed real estate broker or salesperson who advertises to sell, exchange, or lease personally owned real estate shall be identified in the advertisement by name and by indicating that he or she is a real estate broker or salesperson.

81. A is the correct answer. According to ORC 4735.16(B), licensees who list personal property with their broker must disclose in the advertisement (1) the name of the broker under whom they are licensed and (2) the fact that their broker is licensed as such.

82. C is the correct answer. ORC 4735.16(B) requires that the name of the broker to be displayed in equal prominence with the name of the salesperson in the advertisement.

83. A is the correct answer. ORC 4735.16(B) excepts a licensed real estate salesperson from including the broker's name in real estate advertising if the licensee's real property is not listed with his or her broker.

84. D is the correct answer. ORC 4735.16(C) requires real estate brokers and salespersons to furnish a copy of the listing or other agreement to the signor immediately after obtaining his or her signature.

85. A is the correct answer. ORC 4735.16(C) requires every broker's office to prominently display a nondiscrimination statement in the same immediate area as licenses are displayed.

86. A is the correct answer. ORC 4735.16(C) requires that the U.S. Department Housing and Urban Development (HUD) logo appear on all nondiscrimination statements.

87. C is the correct answer. ORC 4735.17(B) requires every nonresident applicant to file an irrevocable consent that suits and actions may be commenced against him or her in any proper court in Ohio.

88. B is the correct answer. According to ORC 4735.18(A), one of the superintendent's primary responsibilities is to investigate the conduct of any real estate licensees.

89. C is the correct answer. ORC 4735.18(A) requires real estate brokers to keep complete and accurate records of all transactions for a period of three years from the date of the transaction or face disciplinary sanctions.

90. C is the correct answer. ORC 4735.19 provides that the Ohio Real Estate Commission may reverse, vacate, or modify an order if an application is filed within 15 days after the mailing of the notice of the order.

91. A is the correct answer. As provided in ORC 4735.18(B), the commission may suspend or revoke the license of the salesperson's broker if the commission finds that the broker had knowledge of the salesperson's unlawful actions.

92. D is the correct answer. ORC 4735.20 states that only licensed real estate brokers, salespersons, and foreign real estate licensees may be paid a commission for real estate services.

93. B is the correct answer. ORC 4735.20(B) states that by virtue of association with a broker or dealer whose license has been suspended or revoked, the salesperson's license is automatically suspended.

94. A is the correct answer. According to ORC 4735.23, commissions for the sale of cemetery lots may be paid in such reasonable amounts as may be fixed by the board of trustees of the cemetery company or association.

95. B is the correct answer. ORC 4735.25(B) requires any person who desires to sell, lease, or deal in any foreign real estate to file an application with the superintendent of real estate.

96. A is the correct answer. As provided in ORC 4735.26(F), the superintendent may require all payments for foreign real estate to be made to a bank in Ohio and to be impounded and held in escrow upon the terms the superintendent reasonably requires.

97. D is the correct answer. ORC 4735.26(B) states that after ten days from the superintendent's order a new application can be filed by the plaintiff for qualification.

98. B is the correct answer. ORC 4735.27(D) requires any applicant who fails the examination twice to wait six months before applying to retake the examination.

99. A is the correct answer. ORC 4735.29 states the license of every foreign real estate dealer and salesperson shall expire on December 31 of each year.

100. C is the correct answer. ORC 4735.32(A)(1) provides that the commission or superintendent may commence an investigation at any time within three years from the date on which an alleged violation of the statute occurred.

101. C is the correct answer. ORC 4735.55(A)(1) requires each written agency agreement to contain an expiration date. Written agency agreements must also contain a statement of fair housing laws, the definition of blockbusting, and a copy of the HUD logo.

102. C is the correct answer. ORC 4735.28(D) provides every salesperson of foreign real estate shall be licensed by the superintendent and shall be employed only by the licensed foreign real estate dealer specified on the salesperson's license.

103. D is the correct answer. ORC 4735.51 provides that an "affiliated licensee" means a real estate broker or a real estate salesperson licensed in Ohio who is affiliated with a brokerage.

104. A is the correct answer. ORC 4735.51(O) states the "subagency" and "subagency relationship" refer to an agency relationship in which a licensee acts for another licensee in performing duties for the client of that licensee.

105. C is the correct answer. ORC 4735.51(F) states that "client" means a person who has entered into an agency relationship with a licensee.

106. B is the correct answer. According to ORC 4735.51(L), "purchaser" means a party in a real estate transaction who is the potential transferee of property. "Purchaser" includes a person seeking to buy property and a person who is seeking to rent or lease property to another.

107. D is the correct answer. ORC 4735.51(K) defines a "management level licensee" as a licensee employed by or affiliated with a real estate broker who has supervisory responsibility over other licensees employed by or affiliated with that real estate broker.

108. C is the correct answer. According to ORC 4735.52, agency relationships are specifically set forth in the statute and the duties of a real estate agent are determined by the common law.

109. A is the correct answer. ORC 4735.55(A)(3), an agency agreement must include a statement defining the practice known as "blockbusting" and stating that it is illegal.

110. B is the correct answer. ORC 4735.54 requires each brokerage to develop and maintain a written company policy that sets forth the types of agency relationships that brokerage members may establish.

111. C is the correct answer. ORC 4735.53(A)(2) establishes four permissible types of agency relationships in Ohio; one is the agency relationship between the licensee and the purchaser.

112. A is the correct answer. ORC 4735.53(A)(3) states that a dual agency relationship is created between the licensee and both the seller and the purchaser.

113. D is the correct answer. ORC 4735.53(A)(3) states that a subagency relationship is created between the licensee and the client of another licensee.

114. D is the correct answer. According ORC 4735.56, a dual agency relationship must be disclosed upfront to all parties.

115. A is the correct answer. ORC 4735.58 states that a licensee acting as a seller's agent shall provide the seller an agency disclosure statement prior to marketing or showing the seller's property.

116. B is the correct answer. ORC 4735.57(A)(2) states that an explanation must be included in the agency disclosure statement that different licensees affiliated with the brokerage might represent the separate interests of a purchaser or a seller in the same transaction.

117. A is the correct answer. ORC 4735.60(A) states a buyer agency disclosure shall take place during the first contact the licensee has with any employee or licensee of the brokerage with which the seller's agent is affiliated; or, if the seller is not represented by a licensee, during the first contact with the seller.

118. B is the correct answer. ORC 4735.62 states that the licensee owes fiduciary duties to a client when representing the client in an agency or subagency relationship.

119. B is the correct answer. ORC 4735.63(2) requires that the licensee shall present any purchase offers to the client in a timely manner.

120. A is the correct answer. ORC 2103.09 abolished the estate of curtesy except those estates by curtesy that have fully vested rights.

121. D is the correct answer. ORC 4735.01(B) excludes cemetery interment rights from the definition of real estate in Ohio.

122. A is the correct answer. ORC 4735.62 describes fiduciary duties generally in agency or subagency relationships including faithful service to the seller.

123. D is the correct answer. ORC 4735.58(e) states that a licensee shall provide the agency disclosure statement prior to submitting an offer to purchase or lease real property.

124. A is the correct answer. ORC 4735.18 states that the commission shall impose disciplinary sanctions against a licensee for violating Ohio license law.

125. A is the correct answer. ORC 4735.08(B) requires that all members or officers who perform functions of real estate brokers must be licensed as brokers.

126. C is the correct answer. ORC 4735.01(6) requires anyone who advertises the lease or rental of real estate to be a licensed broker in Ohio.

127. B is the correct answer. ORC 4735.12(F) provides that $4.00 of application and renewal fees shall be credited to the real estate education and research fund.

128. A is the correct answer. According to ORC 4735.18(A)(17), a licensee may have his or her license revoked for placing a sign on any property offering it for sale or rent without the consent of the owner or the owner's agent.

129. A is the correct answer. ORC 4735.09(C) states that no limit shall be placed on the number of times an applicant may retake the broker's or salesperson's examination.

130. C is the correct answer. ORC 4735.18(A)(11) states that licensees cannot pay commissions or fees to, or divide commissions with, anyone not licensed as a real estate broker.

131. A is the correct answer. ORC 4735.13(F) requires that a broker who is a member or officer of a partnership, association, or corporation as a licensed real estate broker cannot represent anyone except the company the broker works for. A violation of NAR's Code of Ethics does not necessarily equate to a violation of the ORC.

132. A is the correct answer. ORC 4735.18(9) states that a licensee cannot violate or fail to comply or willingly disregard or violate any provisions of Ohio real estate license law.

133. C is the correct answer. ORC 4735.16(C) requires brokers to display the HUD equal housing logo on the brokerage's required nondiscrimination statement.

134. B is the correct answer. ORC 4735.16(B) states that all licensees must be identified in all advertisements for the sale of real property.

135. B is the correct answer. ORC 4735.18(A)(33) prohibits real estate licensees from performing any service for another that constitutes the practice of law, as determined by any court of law.

136. D is the correct answer. ORC 4735.03 states that the governor, with the advice and consent of the senate, shall appoint the five members of the commission.

137. B is the correct answer. ORC 4735.03(A) states that the commission shall adopt Canons of Ethics for the real estate industry.

138. A is the correct answer. ORC 4735.505(A) states the director of commerce may designate any employee of the department as superintendent of real estate.

139. D is the correct answer. ORC 4735.051 states that complaints against licensees must be filed with the DRE and investigated by the superintendent.

140. A is the correct answer. ORC 5302.17 provides that survivorship tenancy is created by conveying the interest in a deed as provided by statute.

141. B is the correct answer. ORC 5307.04 states that a court of common pleas may issue a writ of partition if they find in favor of the plaintiff in an action fee partition.

142. A is the correct answer. ORC 1775.07 defines that partnership property may be held in the partnership's fictitious name or registered name.

143. B is the correct answer. ORC 5311.26(D) & (E) requires that significant financing terms by the developer be disclosed as well as two-year projections of annual expenditures for operations and maintenance costs.

144. C is the correct answer. ORC 319.30 provides for taxes levied upon each tract of land as authorized by law.

145. D is the correct answer. ORC 1311.06 establishes that the filing deadline of an affidavit for a mechanic's lien is 60 days for one- or two-bedroom residences or condominium units.

146. D is the correct answer. ORC 1311.01(C) provides that a properly perfected lien will continue in effect six years after the affidavit is filed.

147. B is the correct answer. ORC 5713.01 states that the county auditor shall appraise for true value all parcels in the county at least once every six years.

148. C is the correct answer. ORC 5721.25 states that at any time prior to the filing of an entry of confirmation, delinquent land may be redeemed by paying all costs and delinquencies in full.

149. A is the correct answer. ORC 319.43 provides that on or before February 15 and August 15 the auditor shall ascertain taxes and assessments to be given to the treasurer for collection.

150. B is the correct answer. ORC 323.13 provides that the county treasurer shall levy a ten percent penalty on outstanding real estate taxes that are past due.

151. A is the correct answer. According to ORC 319.61, special assessments in Ohio are collected in the same way as real estate taxes.

152. A is the correct answer. ORC 2329.02 states that any judgment lien or decree rendered by any court of general jurisdiction shall become a lien on all of the real estate owned by the judgment debtor in that county.

153. B is the correct answer. OAC 5705-3-01(4) provides that the common assessment level of real property is 35 percent of true or market value.

154. D is the correct answer. ORC 5309.97 states that a deed is entitled to be registered where claim of title has been actual, undisputed, and adversely possessed for at 21 years.

155. D is the correct answer. According to ORC 322.02, a county establishes the fee rate for transferring real property interests in the county.

156. A is the correct answer. ORC 5301.01 provides that all deeds must be signed by the grantor, acknowledged and attested to by two witnesses, and certified by a notary public or other designated official.

157. B is the correct answer. ORC 322.02 states that any county may levy and collect a real property transfer tax on each deed conveying real property with the county.

158. A is the correct answer. ORC 2107.03 provides that a valid, executed will must be in writing, signed by the maker (testator), and include the signatures of two witnesses who observed the maker sign the will.

159. B is the correct answer. ORC 319.54 provides that a county may collect up to $4.00 per $100 valuation as a state conveyance fee.

160. B is the correct answer. As outlined in ORC 5309.05, properly transferred deeds of title require the signature of the grantor.

161. A is the correct answer. According to ORC 319.202, the Ohio transfer fee as $.10 per $100 of total consideration based upon the sale of real property.

162. A is the correct answer. ORC 149, also called the Public Records Act, allows anyone to have access to public records including title searches. ORC 5309.38 provides that all records of registered land by the recorder must be open to the public.

163. B is the correct answer. Although not specifically addressed in the ORC, the standard and generally accepted practice is the retention of a title insurance company to issue a title guaranty for a fee.

164. C is the correct answer. According to ORC 5309.03, one of the county recorder's responsibilities is to ensure that all documents and filings meet all legal requirements.

165. B is the correct answer. In Ohio, mortgages must be recorded in order to be recognized by third parties. When mortgages are recorded, they operate as a lien or charge upon the land and bind to it, as provided in ORC 5309.47.

166. B is the correct answer. ORC 5309.34 states that any transferee of registered land shall not be affected with notice, actual or constructive, of any unregistered trust, lien, claim, demand, or interest.

167. B is the correct answer. ORC 5309.30 provides that in order to record a deed it must bear the signature(s) of the grantor(s) and two witnesses with the signature of the notary public who witnessed the grantor(s) signature(s).

168. C is the correct answer. ORC 5309.47 states that mortgages take effect, that is, become a lien upon real property, when they are properly recorded at the county recorder's office.

169. B is the correct answer. ORC 5721.25 allows a foreclosed property to be redeemed at any time prior to the filing of an entry of confirmation of sale by the court.

170. C is the correct answer. According to ORC 1310, leases do not have to be recorded to be valid.

171. B is the correct answer. According to ORC 5321.04 A(8), landlords must provide reasonable notice of their intent to enter at reasonable times. Twenty-four hours is presumed by statute to be reasonable notice in the absence of evidence to the contrary.

172. A is the correct answer. ORC 5321.16 requires landlords to itemize any deductions from the security deposit and return the remainder to the tenant within 30 days of termination of the rental agreement and delivery of possession.

173. B is the correct answer. According to ORC 5321.07(B)(1), when a tenant gives written notice of the violation and the landlord fails to perform, the tenant may deposit all rent that is due with the clerk of court.

174. C is the correct answer. Chapter 4763 of the ORC, pertaining to real estate appraisers, provides for licensure, certification and registration for appraisal services but does not require it. However, FIRREA requires appraisals to be signed by state licensed or certified appraisers.

175. B is the correct answer. According to ORC 4763.01(L), a state-licensed residential real estate appraiser can appraise noncomplex one- to four-unit single-family residential real estate valued at less than $1 million and complex one- to four-unit single-family residential real estate valued at less than $250,000.00.

176. B is the correct answer. Although not stipulated in the ORC, the standard of appraisal practice established in Ohio and most other states is that the appraisal is valid on the day it is made. Also, most lenders will accept the validity of an appraisal for approximately six months from the day it is made unless there are changed conditions.

177. B is the correct answer. Blockbusting is the act of encouraging the sale or rental of property by claiming that the entry of protected persons in a neighborhood will negatively impact property values. ORC 4735.16 states that blockbusting is illegal in Ohio.

178. C is the correct answer. ORC 4112.03 provides that a complaint must be filed within the 12-month period preceding filing with the Ohio Civil Rights Commission.

179. D is the correct answer. Although not codified in the ORC, standards and practices in Ohio generally hold the seller liable for rent expenses for the day of closing. However, this is always subject to agreement between seller and buyer.

180. B is the correct answer. ORC 1311.02 provides lien rights to secure payment against real property owners to the contractor who provides embellishments or improvements to the benefited property.

181. C is the correct answer. ORC 4735.64(A) prohibits a licensee representing a seller from extending an offer of subagency to other licensees.

182. D is the correct answer. ORC 4735.68(A) states that a licensee is not liable for information received from his or her client unless the licensee had actual knowledge that the information was false.

183. B is the correct answer. ORC 4735.69(A) states that a licensee may assist a party who is not the licensee's client by providing general information and referrals to other real estate professionals and support services.

184. C is the correct answer. ORC 4735.67(A) requires a licensee to disclose all material facts to the purchaser when the licensee has actual knowledge pertaining to the physical condition of the property.

185. A is the correct answer. ORC 4735.67(A) states that actual knowledge of material defects shall be implied to the licensee if the licensee acts with reckless disregard for the truth.

186. D is the correct answer. According to ORC 4735.67(E), no one may bring a cause of action against a licensee unless the information was materially inaccurate and was made in bad faith or made with reckless disregard for the truth.

187. A is the correct answer. ORC 4735.67(B) does not require a licensee to discover latent defects in the real property.

188. D is the correct answer. According to ORC 4735.67(B), a licensee is not required to verify the accuracy or completeness of seller statements unless the seller's information should reasonably cause the licensee to question the statements.

189. C is the correct answer. According to ORC 4735.71(A), the seller and the buyer must have full knowledge and consent in writing to dual representation.

190. D is the correct answer. ORC 4735.71(A) states that if, after consent is obtained, there is a material change in the information disclosed to the purchaser and seller, the licensee shall disclose such change of information to both parties, at which time they can revoke their consent.

191. A is the correct answer. While a dual agency disclosure statement is usually provided when it is determined that a dual agency relationship exists, ORC 4735.71(B) requires that the disclosure form must be signed and dated prior to the signing of any offer to purchase or lease real estate.

192. C is the correct answer. ORC 4735.73 states that the superintendent, with the approval of the Ohio Real Estate Commission, shall establish by rule the dual agency disclosure statement.

193. B is the correct answer. According to ORC 4735.73(H), the dual agency disclosure statement must specify the source of compensation to the real estate broker.

194. A is the correct answer. ORC 4735.74(A) states that a licensee owes a duty of accounting to a client after any contract has terminated or expired.

195. B is the correct answer. ORC 4735.99 states that if an applicant is convicted of a false representation in qualifying foreign real estate he or she is guilty of a felony of the fifth degree and may face a fine up to $2,500.00.

196. C is the correct answer. ORC 4735.74(B)(1) requires the licensee to maintain the duty of confidentiality post-transaction unless the client permits disclosure.

197. D is the correct answer. ORC 4735.73(F) defines "material relationship" as any actually known personal, familial or business relationship between the brokerage/licensee that could impair the independent judgment of the licensee toward another client.

198. A is the correct answer. As outlined in ORC 4735.72(A)(1), the brokerage/management-level licensees must objectively supervise the affiliated licensees in the fulfillment of their duties and obligations to their respective clients.

199. B is the correct answer. ORC 5301.01 requires that two people observe the signing of the document and sign their names to their attestation of the witnessed signature.

200. C is the correct answer. ORC 5301.011 provides that any interest in real property shall contain a reference by volume and page to the record of the deed or other recorded instrument.

201. A is the correct answer. According to ORC 5301.47(E), "root of title" is the conveyance that purports to create the interest claimed and is the basis for the marketability of title.

202. D is the correct answer. ORC 5301.47(E) states that the effective date of the "root of title" is the date on which it is recorded.

203. B is the correct answer. ORC 5301.48 states that an unbroken chain of title of record to any interest in land for 40 years or more has a marketable record title.

204. C is the correct answer. ORC 5301.52(B) states that any notice shall be filed for record in the office of the recorder of the county or counties where the land described is situated.

205. C is the correct answer. According to ORC 5302.17, a statutory tenancy deed creates a survivorship tenancy in the grantees, and upon the death of any of the grantees, vests the interest of the decedent in the survivor, survivors, or his, her, or their separate heirs and assigns.

206. A is the correct answer. ORC 5302.30(C) requires every person who intends to transfer any residential real property to deliver a signed and dated copy of the completed form to each prospective transferee or the transferee's agent.

207. D is the correct answer. According to ORC 5302.30(D), the real property disclosure form constitutes a statement of the conditions of the property and of information concerning the property actually known by the transferor.

208. B is the correct answer. According to ORC 5302.30(F)(1), a transferor is not liable in damages if the error or omission of any information on the disclosure form was not within the transferor's actual knowledge.

209. A is the correct answer. According to ORC 5302.30(K)(3)(a), a transferee has three business days from receipt of a property disclosure form in which to rescind the property transfer agreement (sales contract).

210. C is the correct answer. ORC 5302.30(D) states that the property disclosure form shall be designed to allow the transferor to disclose material matters relating to physical condition of the property such as structural problems like a leaky roof.

211. B is the correct answer. As outlined in ORC 5309.93, a lien becomes effective against registered land when it is noted upon the registered certificate of title.

212. C is the correct answer. ORC 5310.02 states that all liens and memorials recorded on title prior to subsequent transfers take priority over those transfers.

213. B is the correct answer. ORC 5310.07 states that if a person, without negligence on his or her part, suffers any loss of interest in land through fraud, error, omission, mistake or misdescription based on recording of title may bring a court action to seek compensation from the assurance fund.

214. D is the correct answer. ORC 5310.11 states that any action to recover from the assurance fund cannot be more than the fair market value of real estate at the time the plaintiff suffered the loss, damage, or deprivation.

215. B is the correct answer. ORC 5310.36 provides that after a cost/benefit review and evaluation by the board of county commissioners, the board may abolish land registration (Torrens land) in the county.

216. D is the correct answer. ORC 5310.41 requires abolished land registration and instruments for its conveyance or encumbrance to be recorded in the traditional recordation system, not in the land registration system.

217. D is the correct answer. ORC 5313.02(C) states that the vendor shall file the land installment contract within 20 days after both parties have signed and dated the contract.

218. B is the correct answer. ORC 5321.07(B)(1) states that a tenant may deposit all rent that is due and thereafter becomes due the landlord with the clerk of the municipal or county court.

219. C is the correct answer. ORC 5321.07(B)(3) states that the tenant has three options, one of which is to terminate the rental agreement.

220. D is the correct answer. According to ORC 5321.07(C), rent withholding does not apply to a landlord who rents out three or fewer dwelling units and who provides tenants with written or verbal notice that withholding rent is not an option.

221. C is the correct answer. According to ORC 5321.13, no agreement to pay the landlord's or tenant's attorney's fees shall be recognized in any residential rental agreement or any other agreement between landlord and tenant.

222. B is the correct answer. ORC 5321.04(A)(6) requires the landlord to supply the tenant a reasonable amount of hot and cold running water.

223. D is the correct answer. ORC 330.212 allows any permanently sited manufactured home to be located in any district or zone where single-family homes are permitted.

224. C is the correct answer. ORC 317.08 requires the county recorder to keep six separate sets of records, including a record of plats.

225. A is the correct answer. ORC 319.30 requires the county auditor to compile tax statements and mail them to every owner of record of real property.

226. D is the correct answer. ORC 322.02 allows any board of county commissioners in Ohio to levy a real property transfer tax to provide additional revenue.

227. C is the correct answer. ORC 519.14(B) states that a township board of zoning appeals will issue, upon appeal, variances from the terms of the zoning resolution.

228. A is the correct answer. ORC 709.13 states that a municipal corporation may enlarge its limits by annexing contiguous territory.

229. B is the correct answer. ORC 711.001 defines a plat as a map of a tract or parcel of land.

230. A is the correct answer. ORC 713.13 states that if either party is especially damaged by the zoning violation either party may institute a suit for injunction to prevent or terminate such violation.

231. C is the correct answer. ORC 1311.02 allows a subcontractor, laborer, or materialman to file a mechanic's lien to secure a payment for the improvement.

232. D is the correct answer. ORC 1311.06 states that the filing of an affidavit for a mechanic's lien must be filed within 60 days from the date on which the last labor or material was furnished.

233. C is the correct answer. ORC 1322.02 requires a mortgage broker to obtain a certificate of registration from the superintendent of financial institutions.

234. D is the correct answer. ORC 1322.8 states that a mortgage broker is not entitled to a fee until the proceeds of the mortgage loan have been disbursed to or on behalf of the buyer.

235. A is the correct answer. ORC 1322.09 requires mortgage brokers to include the certificate of registration number in any advertisements relating to mortgage broker services.

236. B is the correct answer. ORC 1322.10 provides that after notice and an opportunity for a hearing, the superintendent of financial institutions may issue disciplinary actions.

237. C is the correct answer. ORC 1337.01 states that a power of attorney for the conveyance of real property must be signed, attested, acknowledged, and certified.

238. C is the correct answer. ORC 1747.03(A) states that before transacting real estate business in Ohio, the real estate investment trust shall file a report with the office of the Ohio Secretary of State.

239. B is the correct answer. ORC 1923.01(B) states that a forcible entry and detains action shall be brought within two years after the cause of action accrues.

240. D is the correct answer. ORC 4763.05(B) requires a certified or licensed residential real estate appraiser to have at least two years of real estate appraisal experience or its equivalent.

241. B is the correct answer. ORC 4763.02 states that the real estate appraisal board will consist of five members, appointed by the governor and confirmed by the senate.

242. B is the correct answer. ORC 4763.07(A) requires the real estate appraisal certificate holder and licensee to complete 14 hours of continuing education within the first year and 14 hours every year thereafter.

243. A is the correct answer. ORC 5713.01(A) states that the county auditor shall be the assessor of all the real estate in his or her county for taxation purposes.

244. C is the correct answer. ORC 1301:1-4-10 requires the seller to sign the residential property disclosure form.

245. A is the correct answer. ORC 1301:5-3-03 states that any name proposed for use by an individual, partnership, association, or corporation shall be approved by the superintendent.

246. C is the correct answer. According to ORC 1301:5-7-02(E), a classroom clock hour consists of at least 60 minutes.

247. D is the correct answer. As provided in ORC 303.022, the board of County Commissioners may establish or modify planned-unit developments through a county zoning resolution or amendment.

248. B is the correct answer. ORC 5321.05(1) states that a tenant who is a party to a rental agreement shall keep the part of the premises that he or she occupies and uses safe and sanitary.

249. C is the correct answer. ORC 5321.17(C) provides that the landlord or tenant may terminate or fail to renew a month-to-month tenancy by giving notice to the other at least 30 days prior to the periodic rental date.

250. A is the correct answer. ORC 5321.17(C) provides that the periodic tenancy or other rental agreement may be terminated three days after giving notice.